Clyde AND Claudette's Crew

Clyde AND Claudette's Crew

IT ALL ADDS UP!

......at least the way I see it

SIMONE DIANE

XULON PRESS

Xulon Press
2301 Lucien Way #415
Maitland, FL 32751
407.339.4217
www.xulonpress.com

Paperback ISBN-13: 978-1-66285-772-0
Ebook ISBN-13: 978-1-66285-773-7

Dedication

This project is dedicated to my mother, Claudette Colbert Dennis, and is in loving memory of my father, Clyde Lee Dennis, Jr. . I am thankful and grateful to God for both of my parents and have nothing but love, respect, and admiration for them in bigger doses as the years go by. Thank God my mother saw fit to introduce me to God all those years ago. I know that I am just truly blessed!

As my niece so poignantly pointed out, our last family gathering before the world was shut down due to COVID-19 was in honor of our mom/granny/queen and undeniably our matriarch's eighty-fourth birthday. The gathering was on Saturday, March 7, 2020. The nation was halted due to the coronavirus six days later. Although the idea of this publication was conceived during the lockdown, its birth didn't happen until a couple of years later.

Chapter 1

Along this journey called life, we become the person we were intended to be. Life is finite, but legacies are infinite. Our parents were Clyde (affectionately called Poo-Poo by me for some reason) and Claudette (whose personality is so big that I sometimes refer to her as moma since she signs birthday cards, gifts, etc as such although I tend to write momma, mom and our Matriarch). Go figure. Both were born and raised in Conroe, Texas. When I was twenty something years old Poo-Poo said to me, "Pick my brain," on a day when he was feeling pretty good although terminally ill. He sat at his writing desk, aka the kitchen table, and looked out onto the backyard. I did not want to talk about nor think about him not being here with us, so I did not accept his invitation to that conversation or question/answer session.

I learned so much from our parents. I'm randomly reminded of lessons learned while growing up in our family home. In many instances, the best of those lessons learned were not even tagged as learning opportunities as far as I knew. And of course, many of those lessons were such game changers that they have been recycled and passed on to my daughter.

Me not accepting my father's invitation to engage in that conversation that day is one life lesson that begs to be shared: you don't have to accept every invitation that's extended to you.

Poo-Poo was the oldest of his parents' offspring. His parents had three daughters and two sons. My Aunt China is the last living member of that immediate family. That was then; this is now. I have often wondered what valuable information I might have gleaned that day from my father who was such a "think outside the box" kind of man. Nowadays, there are a lot of spotlights being shone on the first Black man or woman to do this or that. I've got to admit that it does make one beam with pride, stand taller, and walk with confidence to hear of such accomplishments when the accolades are attached to someone in your circle. Well, here's one for the books. One interesting thing about our father is that he was the first Black disc jockey in a regular weekly time slot on the country music radio station KIKK out of Pasadena, Texas. This was back in the seventies. I remember my mother gathering us around the radio early in the morning at some awkward hour to hear Poo-Poo's voice. She was so proud of him.

I don't have as many memories of him as I have been able to store up of our matriarch. Two things that I do recall being big deals with Poo-Poo were table etiquette and, omg, that ladies, rather young or old, were not to be seen in public with a roller in their hair! (Not even that one roller for the bang!)

One fond memory is one of my first open house as a classroom teacher. The cool thing was that my parents joined me.

Even before the annual "Take Your Child to Work" day had been introduced, I took my parents to my workplace. I have no idea whose idea it was, but it was fun, and my folks enjoyed it.

Now a memory that is memorable, although it was not at all pleasant, was of Poo-Poo getting upset. He was upset with my mother for telling an approximately ten-year-old me that I had been mistakenly given to them in a hospital mix-up at birth. She asked if I wanted to stay with them or go to live with my "real parents." Whew!

An additional memory is of me being congratulated at our church the Sunday after my parents had gotten the news that they were going to be grandparents again! The baby would be my first and only child. Well, my happy father had shared the news at Bible study! My father had only recently accepted Christ as his Savior and joined church with the family.

Also I recall dealing with my usual beginning of new school year scratchy throat that came with my new group of lovely scholars. I wasn't feeling the best. Poo-Poo kindly reminded me that I probably shouldn't take over the counter medicine because it could harm the unborn baby. What!?

The last notable memory as I take you down memory lane is of the last time I saw Poo-Poo. I'd gone to sit with him after teaching school. I remember seeing the radiant sun through the window as I entered the room. As usual, I watceh *Oprah* as he slept off and on. Soon after my arrival, his dinner was brought in. That day, I fed him for the first time ever. We communicated nonverbally and even almost laughed together about the rate at which he wanted his food. First, I was feeding him too slowly, and so he'd smack his lips for more. Then at one point he let me know that I could slow down a bit. Maybe it was the other way around. As Poo-Poo dozed off and on, I thought about how important the doctors, nurses and all members of the hospital staff were. I could only hope my career choice and how I went about it would make a positive difference in the lives of my students, their famililies, my co-workers and everyone else that I came in contact with at the workplace. By the time the show was over and as I prepared to leave, there was the most beautiful sunset I had ever seen. The next morning, Poo-Poo passed away. I was the last person in our family to see him alive. The memory of our last evening with me feeding my father and the breathtaking sunset has been a sweet reminder of how everything happens according to God's divine design and how precious life is.

As God would have it, Poo-Poo never got to see the grand-child that he'd announced and cared about even before she was born. He passed a couple of months before the beautiful baby girl was born.

When Poo-Poo passed away, our moma was left to single-handedly lead the family. Four of the five of their offspring were young adults living on our own. Our parents already had six grandchildren, who headed up that second line of "the crew". Of course, our Matriarch rose to the occasion.

Chapter 2

Now some interesting things about our matriarch: Her parents allowed her to drink beer and smoke cigarettes at home as early as age twelve, so the story goes. Our matriarch has lived longer than anyone in her family. By God's grace, she's now eighty-six years young! Our matriarch's parents were Zorah Beatrice Josephine McCowan Williams Jefferson and Homer (Mack) Williams. Her stepfather, and our "granddaddy", was Moses Jefferson. She had one sister, Emma Francis Jones, and two brothers, Robert Henry Williams and Eddie Roy Scott. She would drink one can of beer over the course of about a week while we were growing up.

Our mother would work outside the home intermittently during our formative years while Poo-Poo was the constant bread winner. I loved those times when she was between jobs. It felt so good to come from school to the house that couldn't keep the smell of delicious home cooked meals from creeping outside to greet us as we walked up the driveway.

I remember my moma convincing Poo-Poo and then spearheading the actual process of buying me a brand new shininy chocolate brown Toyota Corolla when I graduated from high school!

Our mother ran Granny Camp for two weeks during the summer like a drill sergeant. The children couldn't wait to get there. My mother is the only grandparent my thirty-something year old daughter ever had!

My mom is a real trooper. I can recall a time when our Matriarch was sad and said that all of her friends had passed away. But by the grace of God I saw her make new friends and grow new friendships which have given her great joy!

Several of my friends and associates have spent time with her on several occasions. Now when I speak to them, they will ask how she's doing and what hilarious thing she might have said or done since our last chat. One friend of mine, or of the family as the relationship has grown to be, calls our Matriarch about as often she calls me. They will chat for hours. This young lady once threw me off by answering the phone when I called my mother's house. Our Matriarch is quite endearing.

Chapter 3

During the worldwide pandemic due to COVID-19, there's been a lot of talk about essential workers. Well, as it turns out, not only are we essential in and of our family, but those two individuals produced some bonified essential workers. That's good stuff!

There was an entrepreneurial spirit in all of us. However, the number one goal was to have respectable and reliable sources of income. Those respectful and reliable sources provide comfortable lives. My mother and father are responsible for having put together a solid crew. Between our parents' offspring and the grandchildren, there have been career choices that run the gamut through the alphabet! I am grateful for the kind of individuals God has allowed us to be and is allowing us to become.

Many members of "the crew" earn a living by doing what we enjoy as we provide services to make peoples' lives fuller, safer, and more enjoyable. Some can bring a baby into the world, and one can do a stellar job of taking care of final arrangements when that time comes. Additionally, there are those who've chosen careers of many of those essential jobs needed between the beginning and the end of the life cycle.

That's not all. Not only do we have the young ones whose vocations have yet to be determined, but there's also those of us who are positioning ourselves for our second act. All proof that the legacy will continue. It has been instilled in us that anything worth having is worth waiting and working for. That, my friend, is key. Planning doesn't guarantee that it will happen, but not planning usually guarantees that it (whatever the desired outcome is) won't. Proper planning prevents piss-poor performance. I came across this message during my classroom teacher days. That phrase just spoke to me. It has stayed with me.

My career choice was the "mother of all professions," that of an educator. I learned as much from my profession as my students learned from me. As a matter of fact, everything that I ever needed to know about people and life, I learned or gained a better understanding of while teaching school. It's true that people don't always remember what you say, but they'll never forget how you made them feel. Nor do people care about what you know until they know that you care. Oh, teachers don't have too many times to be ill-prepared before they lose all credibility, respect, and control. But God will provide. He knows what's best and will take care of His own.

It wasn't that I didn't already know His power, however I was young and had lived a sheltered life when I started teaching. But from day one, I felt His presence in the classroom with me. There I was, a twenty-three-year-old who'd finished student teaching on Friday and showed up to teach my own class the following Monday morning. It was December, and those students had already run off four substitute teachers since the school year started! The fact that I was to work only two weeks before a two-week Christmas break was truly a godsend. Within the first few weeks as a classroom teacher, I realized that we humans are more alike than we are different. I did return after the break and completed the spring semester. That was another godsend in that I only had to live with my new teacher mistakes for five months instead of the usual nine months. Won't He do it? Fast forward many years. I've retired, and we are in the middle of a world-wide pandemic. I see daily reminders that we humans are still more alike than we are different, for example, the interior of our homes with pillows galore in the background on Zoom meetings.

For thirty-three years, God kept me in my travels to and from work and while in the classroom. Then, unbeknownst to me, I even have neighbors who were retired and stayed at home most of the time. That really worked for me and made me feel safe knowing others are within earshot. Thanks to God's amazing grace and my loving husband, John Wesley Massingill I have enjoyed five years of retirement already.

I will say that the biggest drawback to being a classroom teacher is that all too often one never gets to see the fruit of the labor. To this end, there was certainly a village in my case. I could never name all my village people here. Please accept my apologies. Know that your efforts did not go unnoticed. Thanks! However, I would like to say thank you to the best third-grade teacher in the world, Mrs. H. Thank you to the best college math professor ever, Dr. D. B. A big thanks to Ms. G.W., my student teacher supervisor. Thanks to Mrs. J. T., my mentor. Lastly, and of utmost importance, a huge THANKS to the best pastor on this side of heaven, Rev. J.H.B., Jr. as well as my entire FFBC church family!!!

Chapter 4

Thinking about professions, vocations, and career choices makes one think about jobs of the past that are obsolete. For example, an elevator operator. That was a person responsible for transporting people through different floors of an establishmnet by operating the buttons or levers. (Moma, perhaps you'll enjoy reminiscing about these ideals and your best memories of some with friends or our young family members.) Additionally, there are some jobs that will disappear in the next couple of years since our society is becoming more and more technology driven.

Our younger "crew members" may be wondering, "So, what are some other options and ideals for career choices?" The options are endless. There are those everyone knows about and/or can imagine right now, as well as anything that is not known/heard of but can be imagined by you! Everyone should choose the path that catapults them into the space where they are the best version of themselves! Do what makes you happy most days as you earn the means to support a great life! Just don't get so busy making a living that you forget to live. Guys, tap into your resources, which includes all of us.

I avail myself and share all I've gleaned over the years with those who ask or are in my care. Erica Simone, my dear daughter, you are the apple of my eye. You are hands down my best gift ever from the absolute best gift giver there is. I'm so grateful that God has allowed both of us to live long enough for you to think I'm grand again! Things have even gotten to the point that you intentionally listen to what I say and even ask me for advice. Wow! It is my pleasure to share this time and pour all I've learned into you, my dear! I have learned so much from you as well.

To my fellow C and C crew members,

My hope is that each of you has found/will find that path that brings you much satisfaction and happiness. I am proud of who God has allowed us to become. You should be proud, too! Let us be present for each other and represent well! I pray that regardless of where you are in life, you will always fully rely on God! I love you all!

To Our Matriarch,

Moma, you've got to know that your quick wit and sense of humor are second to none. Oh, the things you come up with to say! And to think that you don't seem to give it much thought…it comes up and out and can be just outright hilarious! You (and all your little sayings) are one for the books. But that's another story. Over the years, I have grown to recognize and appreciate the upbringing, traditions, and opportunities that were afforded to me and my siblings by y'all. You all did well Moma!

It has been and is my absolute pleasure to avail myself to you! This gift of time from God has allowed me to spend precious moments with you at the center with all your cute peeps as you all play cards and celebrate birthdays; as we slide in just in time for your doctor appointments because one of us just tends to be on island time all the time; as we eat breakfast after almost every outing but still have you back to your house before the hustle and bustle starts for the day; the shopping trips; the runs to the dressmaker for alterations and as we visit different friends of yours and mine. My favorite has been those endearing full-circle moments when you'd ask me to take you somewhere. The cherry on top was when you'd ask me if one (or more) of your friends could ride with us. I sincerely thank God that He's allowed my retirement to coincide with your golden years!

Thanks Moma
Love, Bo

This is
THE END
of this book but not the end of this story.

WITH GOD AS THE HEAD OF OUR
FAMILY AND WE THE BODY, THROUGH
"THE CREW,"
THE STORY IS TO BE CONTINUED.
THIS LEGACY IS ONE THAT WILL LIVE ON!

CPSIA information can be obtained
at www.ICGtesting.com
Printed in the USA
BVHW040321070223
657956BV00014B/38